Frontispiece Toco Toucan (No. 26)

1 Edward, 13th Earl of Derby (No. 1)

2 Edward Lear (No. 2)

MERSEYSIDE COUNTY COUNCIL

An Exhibition of Watercolours belonging to the Earl of Derby

WALKER
ART
GALLERY
LIVERPOOL 1975

EDWARD LEAR & KNOWSLEY

SBN 90153431 5

Printed by Elliott Bros. & Yeoman Ltd., Speke, Liverpool L24 9JL
Type: Imprint (Series 101 and 310), 10 on 11
Text and Plates: Super Dual Proven White Art 140 gsm
Cover: Keays—Packwood Lemon 280 gsm
Blocks: Gilchrist Bros., Leeds

Foreword

IT is with great pleasure that we mount this exhibition of bird and landscape drawings by Edward Lear at Knowsley by the kind invitation of the Right Hon. The Earl of Derby, M.C.

It was at the invitation of Lord Derby's ancestor, the 13th Earl, in 1832 that the young Lear spent several happy years drawing the wild life in the famous menagerie there, for the advancement of science. It was there that he discovered his own talent for devising Nonsense Verse for the amusement of the grandchildren after dinner, and it was due to his enlightened patron and his family that Lear afterwards embarked on his fascinating travels through Europe and the East as far as India, recording the scenery of so many hot and romantic places in a crisp linear shorthand style to be developed afterwards into richly coloured compositions.

Many of these landscapes were also acquired by the Earls of Derby and the present Earl has generously enabled us to see them alongside a selection of the original zoological drawings. The Nonsense drawings alone are missing, having passed to other branches of the family long ago.

From the Derby Museum bequeathed to Liverpool by the 13th Earl, we are able to show some few of the original specimens which Lear drew in the menagerie. We should particularly like to thank the Director and the Department of Zoology in Merseyside County Museums, for their generous assistance in making this possible and for so much valuable help in the catalogue. At the same time we should like to thank the Liverpool City Librarian for generously lending the rare copies of Lear's two most famous bird books, in which some of the drawings are published.

The Earl of Derby, like all his family, has always taken a personal interest in Merseyside. We would like to thank him most sincerely for his gesture which we know will be fully appreciated by the visitors to our Gallery.

COUNCILLOR B. SHAW
Chairman
Arts and Culture Committee
Merseyside County Council

Cover from the first Book of Nonsense

Introduction

EDWARD Lear, famous for his limericks and nonsense verse and a successful landscape painter in watercolour, began his career as a zoological draughtsman. He was fortunate to find early in life an important patron in Edward Lord Stanley, to whom he was introduced in 1832. At the time Lear was working at the London Zoo in Regent's Park where he had been engaged by the Zoological Society to make drawings of the parrots, forty-two of which he later published in a lavish folio volume, *Illustrations of the Family of Psittacidae* (1832). Lord Stanley, then President of the Zoological Society, saw Lear at work and was so impressed by the quality of his drawings that he invited him to his home at Knowsley Hall near Liverpool to draw the birds and animals in the superb private menagerie that he had established there.

Unlike his father, the 12th Earl, whose enthusiasm for animals had centred almost exclusively on the breeding and training of fighting cocks and race horses (it was he who instituted the famous Derby and Oaks meetings at Epsom), the interests of Lord Stanley, who succeeded as 13th Earl in 1834, were of a quieter, more scholarly nature. From his youth he had made a detailed study of birds and animals and in adult life he directed his attentions to scientific research and collecting and breeding rare and exotic species of the type that would be ornamental or useful if successfully naturalized in this country. A keen and dedicated naturalist, for whom ornithological pursuits became the ruling passions of his life, he also set about extending the small menagerie and aviaries at Knowsley, which formerly were no larger than those of any other fine stately home of the period, and dedicated many years of labour and a considerable fortune to their upkeep and improvement.

As a result of his singleminded determination and zeal the living collection at Knowsley grew in his lifetime to become the largest and finest of its kind in England, rivalled only by the zoological collections of Earl Fitzwilliam at Wentworth or Sir Robert Heron, a Lincolnshire Baronet, whose passion for animals was second only to Lord Derby's.

In its heyday close on 100 acres of land at Knowsley and vast expanses of water were given over to the various enclosures, paddocks, aviaries and plantations that the animals and birds required. At one period some thirty attendants, under the supervision of John Thompson, were mentioned in Lord Derby's pay lists and at the time of his death in 1851 he was in touch with over twenty agents all over the world whose task it was to locate and supply him with new specimens, both for the museum at Knowsley and for the live collection.

To augment these specimens, Lord Derby also financed several expeditions: to the South and West coasts of Africa, to Honduras, to the Hudson Bay Territories and, closer to home, in Germany, Norway and Sweden. As a result innumerable valuable specimens and several species altogether new to science found their way to England, though not all to Liverpool, for all the larger animals went either to the British Museum or to the Zoological Society. Nevertheless, when the living collection was auctioned after Lord Derby's death in 1851, it consisted of no fewer than 345 mammals (comprising 94 species) and 1272 birds (comprising 318 species), of which as many as 756 individuals had been bred at Knowsley.

The list of dead specimens in the Derby Museum, which was bequeathed to Liverpool in 1851 and is now part of Merseyside County Museums, is equally impressive. Among its more remarkable possessions there are numerous type specimens, the actual birds from which a new species was first described to science, and countless varieties of birds and animals now extremely rare in the wild or actually extinct. Some exceptional early items were brought home on Captain Cook's ships.

It is clear that what prompted Lord Derby to employ Lear at Knowsley was above all the thought that his drawings would substantially aid the identification of specimens in his menagerie and thus facilitate their subsequent scientific classification. Indeed, there is evidence that he put them to this very purpose, for many are inscribed in Lord Derby's hand with scientific names that were devised long after Lear had drawn them. In some instances, in fact, Lear had recorded birds which were completely unknown to science, that is to say, specimens which only much later were recognised as the types.

Lear arrived at Knowsley in 1832, shortly after publication of the *Psittacidae* (on the merits of which he was nominated an associate of the Linnaean Society), and worked there intermittently until July 1837. He was unable to concentrate all his energies on the Derby menagerie for he was already committed to providing John Gould with illustrations for his *Family of Toucans* (1834) and *Birds of Europe* (1837) and this obligation necessitated regular visits to London. In July and August 1835 he was again away from Knowsley on a walking holiday in Ireland and in 1836 he spent several weeks in late summer touring and sketching in the Lake District. But all the months spent at Knowsley were passed in feverish activity and during the five years he was there he produced an astonishing array of exquisite bird and animal drawings, some done from live, others from dead specimens. The finest of these were published in 1846, faithfully lithographed by J. W. Moore, in the first of two volumes entitled *Gleanings from the Menagerie and Aviary at Knowsley Hall*, a work financed by Lord Derby and edited by Dr. John Gray of the British Museum, who also selected the plates.

The best of Lear's zoological illustrations for the 13th Earl (now divided between Knowsley and the Wood Library of the McGill University, Montreal) are perhaps as remarkable for their sense of design as for their verisimilitude and flawless anatomical precision, qualities which at moments reveal Lear as the equal of his American near contemporary John James Audubon. Indeed, by and large, Lear's drawings are considerably more convincing than his and decidedly more lifelike than those of most earlier bird illustrators. This is principally explained by the fact that in the main Lear drew from live specimens (one of the very first artists ever to do so), whereas his predecessors had invariably based their studies solely on stuffed birds and skins or, in Audubon's case, on birds that had been observed in their natural state but were nevertheless killed before being drawn.

His bird and animal drawings aside, Lear's stay at Knowsley was of crucial importance to the development of his versatile career in two notable respects. It was there, as he entertained Lord Derby's grandchildren in their nursery after dinner, that he first became aware of his extraordinary talents as a writer and illustrator of limericks and nonsense verse, a discovery which led in 1846 to the publication of his justly famous and ever popular *Book of Nonsense*—composed largely of ideas originally conceived to amuse the children of the Derby household—and to the many other nonsense poems and alphabets that followed in its train. At Knowsley too he gained many important introductions to "half the fine people of the day", as he called them, men and women of substance who were later to prove, like the Earls of Derby themselves, true and generous friends when Lear had pictures to sell or was in need of fresh commissions.

But in 1837, in ill health and already suffering from impaired eyesight after the months of close, detailed observation his work at Knowsley had entailed, Lear made up his mind to give up zoological illustration and determined to devote the rest of his life to landscape painting. What he longed for most was to embark for the drier, sunnier climate of the South and to have an opportunity to paint unworried by financial cares. This was eventually realised only with the kindly support he received from Lord Derby and his nephew, Robert Hornby, who gave Lear not only the greatest encouragement in his new venture but provided help of the most practical sort, by putting up between them all the funds that he needed to be able to live and work for a time in Italy. It was a gesture typical of the 13th Earl.

Lear set out for Rome in July 1837 and with the exception of a long stay in England from 1849 until 1853 and a succession of considerably shorter visits to this country he remained abroad for the rest of his life, settling first in Italy, where he stayed for ten years, and afterwards in Corfu, Cannes and finally San Remo, where he built his house, the Villa Emily.

In common with many of his generation Lear was an ardent and indefatigable traveller and after 1837 he was almost constantly on the move, sketching first in Europe and the Mediterranean and then, like Holman Hunt and Thomas Seddon and David Roberts before them, in Egypt and throughout the Near East, often in the most hazardous terrain and, despite several unpleasant encounters, with conspicuous disregard for his own safety. In the beginning he journeyed alone or in company with a friend; later in life he engaged a manservant, Giorgio Kokali, who acted as his faithful companion and porter wherever they went. Lear once confessed that he wanted to "topographise all the journeyings of my life" and scarcely a day went by, hardly an excursion was made without Lear recording the details in his sketch-book or sitting down in front of nature to draw the scene before him, most often with pen and ink and rapidly applied colour washes. Later in his studio he transformed these hasty sketches into highly finished watercolours and oil paintings or produced from them the lithographic plates which he used to illustrate his numerous travel books.

Despite his living almost constantly abroad, Lear always kept in close contact through letters with his many friends at home including, of course, the 13th Earl of Derby, with whom he maintained a regular correspondence throughout his life. Whenever Lear returned to England he made a particular point of visiting Knowsley and his appearance there was greeted at all times with the warmest reception. In 1841 he spent much of August at Knowsley and in 1849 one of the first calls he made on his return to England was to "Mr Hornby & Lord Derby (whom)

I found just as ever, though 72 & 75 . . . Certainly English people do go on with friendship just where they left off, as you go on with a book at the page you last read."

Lear's lifelong associations with Knowsley survived even after the death in 1851 of his dear friend, the 13th Earl. Letters continued to pass between Lear and Knowsley and in 1853 the 14th Earl demonstrated his own partiality for Lear's work by asking him to do a painting of Windsor Castle. It was the first commission he had been given since his return to England. Likewise, the 15th Earl in his turn proved as ardent an enthusiast for Lear's pictures as his predecessors had been. As a child Lear had entertained him with his nonsense in the nursery at Knowsley; now in 1869 he wrote asking a favour. Could he paint a picture for him? In return Lear received "a wonderfully kind & nice letter, wishing for a Corfu—100£." In due course the 15th Earl bought other paintings from the artist, including a large oil of Bonifazio in Corsica and several delightful watercolours. In January 1883 he wrote to Lear: "Come over this spring and bring a room full of work with you. There is space still at Knowsley for a few more of your drawings, though I have a pretty good stock already".

In this way Lear benefited from the sustained patronage of the Earls of Derby throughout successive generations, and he was the first to acknowledge their generosity. "Lord Derby," he wrote in 1883, referring to the 15th Earl, "is always employing me in one way or another, as did his father, his grandfather and his great-grandfather. Fancy having worked for 4 Earls of Derby".

Colin J. Bailey

ACKNOWLEDGEMENTS

For their generous help with the preparation of the entries on the birds and animals included in this exhibition I should like to thank especially Peter Morgan, Keeper of Vertebrate Zoology in the Merseyside County Museums, and his assistant Keeper, Ian Harris, without whose specialist knowledge the first section of this catalogue could not have taken its present form.

C.J.B.

With the exception of Holman Hunt's portrait of Edward Lear, which is the property of the Walker Art Gallery, all exhibits have been lent by the Earl of Derby.
In all cases, dimensions are sight sizes, inches before centimetres, height before width.
The modern taxonomic names of the birds are taken from J. L. Peters' *Check List of the Birds of the World.*

Watercolours distinguished by a † were painted from the type specimens now preserved in the Merseyside County Museums. Those marked with an * were painted from Knowsley specimens, the majority of which now belong to the Merseyside County Museums. The unmarked entries dated 1831 are commoner species which could have been drawn either at Knowsley or, most likely, in London.

Catalogue

1

William Derby (1786–1847) *Plate 1*

Portrait of Edward, 13th Earl of Derby, K.G.

Watercolour and gouache, $10\frac{1}{2} \times 8\frac{1}{5}$ (26·7 × 20·8)
Signed and dated: *W. Derby pinxt 1837.*

Edward Smith-Stanley: born in 1775; married 1798; created Baron Stanley of Bickerstaffe 1832; succeeded to the earldom 1834; created Knight of the Garter 1839; died at Knowsley 1851. Lear's first important patron, he is most famous as the founder of the celebrated zoological collection and scientific library at Knowsley.

Lord Derby is shown seated at a table on which are two books (*Linnaeus* and *Transactions of the Zoological Society*), a plan for the diversion of roads at Knowsley, and a roll inscribed *Drawings, Nat. History, by Edward Lear.* He was a kind, intelligent man described by his amanuensis as "tall and of very active habits, fond of walking and of his gun, but very deaf". Sadly, he became paralysed on his left side shortly after attaining his title.

2

William Holman Hunt (1827–1910)

Portrait of Edward Lear

Plate 2

Black and red chalk, $23\frac{9}{16} \times 18\frac{5}{8}$ (59·7 × 47·2)
Signed in monogram: *W h h* and dated *Nov 7 1857*

Lear met Hunt (whom he always addressed subsequently as *Daddy* or *Pa*) in 1852 when they were introduced by the painter Robert Martineau. Hunt gave Lear considerable technical advice in the matter of oil painting and for a while they lived together at Clive Vale Farm near Hastings, while they both painted in the surrounding countryside. Lear's interest in Pre-Raphaelite working methods and the enthusiasm they shared for travelling abroad established a strong bond between the two men and they remained lifelong friends. On his visit to Egypt in 1854 Lear intended joining up with Holman Hunt but was persuaded to take part in an expedition up the Nile and the meeting never came about.

3

Chestnut Belted Gnateater

Plate 8

Conophaga aurita (Gmelin)

Pen and brown ink, watercolour, and watercolour mixed with gum, heightened with white, $14 \times 9\frac{15}{16}$ (35·5 × 25·3)
Signed and dated: *E. Lear. 1830.*
Inscribed: *Conopophaga aurita South America.* and above this in pencil: *Conopophaga aurita*

This small inhabitant of Colombia and Brazil feeds on insects that it finds amongst the forest undergrowth. The bird figured is a female, the male of the species being distinguished by a blackish head and throat, a difference of colour first noticed in the 1830's.

This is one of several early drawings executed before Lear went to Knowsley and later presented by him to the 13th Earl of Derby.

4

Red Capped Parrot

Purpureicephalus spurius (Kuhl)

Watercolour, and watercolour mixed with gum,
$15\frac{3}{8} \times 11\frac{7}{8}$ (39·1 × 30·2)
Signed and dated: *E. Lear. 1831. Sept. br*
Inscribed: *Platycercus pileatus, Vig. female. Swan River. Drawn from a specimen in the Knowsley Aviaries; and the Original from whence Plate 22 of Lear's Illustrations of Psittacidæ was taken.*

The original study for Plate 22 in *Illustrations of the Family of Psittacidæ.*

When drawn this bird was living in the aviaries at Knowsley. It is an immature specimen of the brightly coloured species called the Red Capped Parrot, which is found in parts of Australia. The specially adapted bill is used for extracting seeds from the pods of eucalyptus trees, on which it feeds.

The inscription on this drawing suggests that Lear had visited Knowsley, if only briefly, as early as 1831, before his formal introduction to Lord Stanley at Regent's Park. However, it should not be assumed that the other zoological illustrations dated 1831 and now in the collection of Lord Derby were necessarily drawn from birds at Knowsley, for the 13th Earl is known to have acquired several of Lear's early bird drawings to add to those he had commissioned from the artist. (Cf. nos. 6, 8 and 10).

5

Dusky Parrot

Plate 3

Pionus fuscus (P. L. S. Müller)

Pen and brown ink, watercolour, and watercolour mixed with gum, $16\frac{3}{8} \times 11\frac{7}{8}$ (41·6 × 30·2)
Signed and dated: *E. Lear. 1831.*
Inscribed: *Psittacus violaceus* (*Bodd*) *South America.*

This parrot belongs to a forest species that is found in South America. Lear could have drawn this bird during his visit to Knowsley in 1831 (see no. 4) since there were three specimens living in the aviary there at that time, but he is more likely to have worked from a bird in the Zoo at Regent's Park.

6

Abyssinian Lovebird†

Agapornis taranta taranta (Stanley)

Pen and brown ink, watercolour, and watercolour mixed with gum, $14\frac{15}{16} \times 12\frac{1}{8}$ (38 × 30·8)
Signed and dated: *E. Lear. 1831*
Inscribed: *Psittacula Tarantæ* (*Stanley*). *Abyssinia. This was drawn from the Original specimen, in the Knowsley Museum* (*MSS. Cat. No. 704.*) *and was the drawing from which Plate 39 of Lear's Illustrations of Psittacidae, was taken.*

The original study for Plate 39 in the *Psittacidæ.*

Lear painted this from a dead specimen that Lord Stanley (later 13th Earl) had acquired in 1812. It was obtained from a Mr. Salt who had been in Abyssinia and had observed the

Lovebird—"the only parrot I saw in Abyssinia"—congregating with others of the species in small groups of four or five.

This watercolour is of particular interest since it records the type specimen, the actual bird from which the species was first described to science in 1814.

7
Great Potoo
Nyctibius grandis Gmelin

Watercolour, watercolour mixed with gum, and traces of pencil, $19 \times 13\frac{3}{4}$ ($48 \cdot 2 \times 35$)
Signed and dated: *E. Lear. del. 1831.*
Inscribed: *Nyctibius grandis, South America.*

The Great Potoo is a nocturnal bird from South America whose feeding habits include perching on a tree stump or fence post and flying out to catch large insects on the wing.

This drawing must have been done somewhere other than at Knowsley since Lord Derby kept no birds of this species there until the late 1830's.

8
Cockatiel
Plate 6
Nymphicus hollandicus (Kerr)

Watercolour, and watercolour mixed with gum, $19\frac{15}{16} \times 13\frac{1}{2}$ ($50 \cdot 6 \times 34 \cdot 3$)
Signed and dated: *E. Lear. 1831*
Inscribed: *Nymphicus Novæ—Hollandiæ (Gmel.). Australia. The Original drawing from which the plate (with alterations) in Lear's Illustrations of Psittacidæ, pl. 27, was taken.*

The original study for Plate 27 in the *Psittacidæ*.

Lear was the first artist accurately to depict both the male and female of this species, a common parrot from Australia, which since the 19th century has become one of the most popular of cage birds. Both a cock and hen of the species are shown here.

9
Lord Derby's Parakeet†
Plate 10
Psittacula derbiana (Fraser)

Pen and brown ink, watercolour, and watercolour mixed with gum, $20\frac{1}{2} \times 12\frac{1}{2}$ ($52 \times 31 \cdot 7$)
Signed: *E. Lear.* and dated *1831*
Inscribed: *Palæornis Derbianus Fraser MSS. India.*

Lord Derby's Parakeet was named by Louis Fraser in 1850 in honour of the 13th Earl for his valuable contributions to ornithology. It is a rare bird occurring only in South China and Tibet, though, as the inscription indicates, it was at one time erroneously thought to inhabit India.

When Lear painted this bird from the Knowsley museum it was the only example of its species to be found in England.

10

Western Rosella

Platycercus icterotis (Kuhl)

Watercolour, and watercolour mixed with gum,
$14\frac{15}{16} \times 11\frac{15}{16}$ (38 × 30·2)
Signed and dated: *E. Lear Septr. 1831*
Inscribed: *female or young male. Stanley Parrakeet Platycercus icterotis (Temm.) Swan River. The Original of Plate 24 of Lear's Illustrations of Psittacidæ.*

The original study for Plate 24 in the *Psittacidæ*.

A native of Australia, this is one of many species of rosella that were kept in the aviaries at Knowsley. This particular species was first described to science in 1820.

11

Golden Parakeet

Aratinga guarouba (Gmelin)

Pen and brown ink, watercolour, and watercolour mixed with gum, heightened with white, $16\frac{3}{16} \times 13\frac{3}{16}$ (41·1 × 33·5)
Signed and dated: *1831. E. Lear.*
Inscribed: *Conurus luteus (Bodd) Brazil.*

It is instructive to compare this early drawing, close in style to Lear's illustrations for the *Psittacidæ*, with his more lifelike and accomplished rendering of a Golden Parakeet done five years later (no. 27).

12

Red Shafted Flicker*

Plate 4

Colaptes cafer (Gmelin)

Pen and brown ink, watercolour, and watercolour mixed with gum, heightened with white, $16\frac{3}{4} \times 12\frac{5}{8}$ (41·6 × 32·1)
Signed: *E. Lear.*
Inscribed: *Colaptes rubricatus (Licht.) Monterey. The upper figure appears, with alterations, to have been the Original of Plate 9 of the Appendix to Capt. Beechey's Voyage.*

Possibly the original study for Plate 9 in the appendix to *The Zoology of Captain Beechey's Voyage* (1839), to which Lear contributed illustrations.

These two birds were bought as dead specimens from John Gould in 1832. They form part of a complex group of Woodpeckers (called Flickers in the United States) which have large areas of hybridization, especially along the west coast of North America.

13

Argentine Red Shoveller*

Plate 17

Spatula platalea (Vieillot)

Watercolour, watercolour mixed with gum, and traces of pencil, $7\frac{1}{4} \times 10\frac{15}{16}$ (18·4 × 27·9)
Signed: *E. Lear. del.* and dated *March. 1834.*
Inscribed: *Spatula maculata, (Gould). South America.*

Lord Stanley purchased this as a dead specimen on 8th November 1833 from the same Mr. Mather who earlier that year had supplied him with the *Penelope superciliaris* (no. 17). Mather had obtained this attractively marked duck near Buenos Aires.

14
Chinese Francolin*
Francolinus pintadeanus (Scolopi)

Watercolour, and watercolour mixed with gum,
11 7/16 × 19 3/8 (29·1 × 49·2)
Signed: *Edward. Lear. del.* and dated *1835.*
Inscribed: *Francolinus perlatus,* (*Gmel.*)

These two birds, originally brought to England alive from China, died in the Knowsley aviaries in October 1835. As was invariably the case their skins were then transferred to the Derby Museum.

This species is now also found in Madagascar, Reunion and Mauritius, having been introduced there since the 19th century.

15
Red Legged Seriema* *Plate 9*
Cariama cristata (Linnaeus)

Watercolour, and watercolour mixed with gum,
19 5/16 × 13 9/16 (49·1 × 34·5)
Signed: *E. Lear. del.* and dated *July. 1835.*
Inscribed: *Cariama cristata, Linn. Guiana* (in ink over an identical pencil inscription) and *Dicholophus Cariama* (pencil).

Red Legged Seriemas, although they fly a little, are primarily terrestrial creatures, feeding on small reptiles and mammals. The species is confined to South America and this particular specimen came to Knowsley from Guiana.

16
Rhea
Rhea americana (Linnaeus)

Watercolour, and watercolour mixed with gum,
19 1/8 × 13 3/4 (48·5 × 35·1)
Signed: *Edward Lear. del.* and dated *July. 1835.*
Inscribed: *Rhea Americana* (*Linn*) *East coast of South America. The Original of the plate in the 'Gleanings'* and *S. American Ostrich* (pencil).

The original study for Plate XII in *Gleanings from the Menagerie and Aviary at Knowsley Hall.*

The Rhea is a large, fast running flightless bird from the plains of South America. The 13th Earl made numerous attempts to breed this species at Knowsley and was eventually successful. The following are extracts from his notes: "My Rhea eggs have hatched ill this year; out of twenty-six, twenty-three proved bad, and the other three had dead birds in them. But I have three later still to hatch: I hope they may prove more lucky" (18.9.1845). "The *Rhea Americana* has bred here twice, and at this moment I have, I believe, upwards of forty eggs, laid partly, I believe, by those bred here" (21.7.1846).

17

Rusty Margined Guan*

Penelope superciliaris Temminck

Watercolour, and watercolour mixed with gum,
$12\frac{3}{16} \times 17\frac{5}{8}$ (30·9 × 44·7)
Signed and dated: *Edward Lear. del. July. 1835.*
Inscribed: *Penelope superciliaris, Illiger. Tropical America The Original of the plate in the 'Gleanings'.* (in ink over an identical inscription).

The original study for Plate VIII in the *Gleanings.*

From records which were kept of the acquisitions at Knowsley it is thought that the specimen on which Lear based this watercolour drawing was purchased *dead* from Mr. Mather on 15th January 1833. Dr. John Gray's remark in the preface to the *Gleanings* that "the chief value" of Lear's illustrations "consists in their being accurate representations of *living* specimens" must therefore be regarded with caution.

18

Short Toed Eagle*

Plate 13

Circaëtus gallicus (Gmelin)

Watercolour, and watercolour mixed with gum,
$17\frac{3}{8} \times 13\frac{11}{16}$ (44·1 × 34·7)
Signed and dated: *Edward Lear. del. Sept. 1835.*
Inscribed: *Circaëtus gallicus (Gmel.) Mogadore.*

This was one of the many birds of prey kept by Lord Derby at Knowsley. In the wild its diet consists primarily of snakes, for which reason it is also known as the Serpent Eagle.

19

Red Crowned Parrot*

Plate 5

Poicephalus gulielmi fantiensis Neumann

Watercolour, and watercolour mixed with gum,
$14\frac{7}{8} \times 12\frac{7}{16}$ (37·7 × 31·6)
Signed: *Edward Lear. del.* and dated *Sept. 1835.*
Inscribed: *Psittacus Gulielmi (Jardine) Western Africa.*

This bird died in Lord Derby's aviaries on 24th December 1834. The subspecies to which it belongs comes from the forests of Ghana (formerly the Gold Coast) and in the 19th century it would have been a rare bird to find in a European collection.

20

Stanley Crane*

Plate 12

Anthropoides paradisea (Lichtenstein)

Watercolour, watercolour mixed with gum, and traces of pencil,
$20\frac{1}{16} \times 14$ (51 × 35·5)
Signed: *Edward Lear. del* and dated *Sept. 1835.*
Inscribed: *Stanley Crane Scops Paradisea (Licht.) South Africa The Original of the Plate in the 'Gleanings'.*

The original study for Plate XIV in the *Gleanings.*

In the notes that he made on his living collection the 13th Earl wrote: "I possessed for some years several individuals of that species of the genus *Anthropoides* which my late friend Dr. Latham had done me the honour to distinguish by my name, in consequence of my having had the good fortune to draw his attention to the bird, which I had seen in the Tower of London".

In their day these birds were famous at Knowsley for their splendid courtship dance.

3 Dusky Parrot (No. 5)

4 Red Shafted Flicker (No. 12)

5 Red Crowned Parrot (No. 19)

6 Cockatiel (No. 8)

7 Blue Crowned Parakeet (No. 34)

8 Chestnut Belted Gnateater (No. 3)

9 Red Legged Seriema (No. 15)

10 Lord Derby's Parakeet (No. 9)

11 Golden Parakeet (No. 27)

12 Stanley Crane (No. 20)

13 Short Toed Eagle (No. 18)

14 Abyssinian Touraco (No. 25)

15 Douroucouli or Night Monkey (No. 37)

16 Spectacled Owl (No. 31)

17 Argentine Red Shoveller (No. 13)

18 Malayan Giant Squirrel (No. 40)

19 Olive Grove on Corfu (No. 53)

20 A Rocky Inlet on the Island of Paxos (No. 56)

21 Philae (No. 51)

22 Corfu (No. 52)

23 Ióannina (No. 50)

24 The Forest of Bavella (No. 59)

25 Cattaro (Kotor) (No. 58)

21

Spoon Billed Sandpiper*

Eurynorhynchus pygmeus (Linnaeus)

Watercolour, $10\frac{1}{2} \times 17\frac{7}{8}$ (26·6 × 45·3)
Signed: *Edward Lear. del.* and dated *Nov. 1835.*
Inscribed: *Eurinorhynchus pygmaus*

In the 19th century very few specimens of this unusual wader from Eastern Asia reached Western Europe. Lord Derby, however, managed to procure several for his museum collection.

22

Woodcock and Common Snipe

Scolopax rusticola Linnaeus and Capella gallinago (Linnaeus)

Watercolour, and watercolour mixed with gum, heightened with white, $16\frac{1}{2} \times 10\frac{9}{16}$ (42 × 26·8)
Signed and dated on label: *Mr. Lear./28. Southampton/Decr. 1835.*
Inscribed: *Scolopax rusticola, Linn. British. Scolopax gallinago, Penn.*

These two types of wading bird were frequently shot on the estate at Knowsley where the Woodcock still breeds in reasonable numbers. Several specimens killed in this way were added to the large collection of stuffed birds and skins in the Derby Museum.

This drawing possibly records a Christmas gift to Lear from Lord Derby, sent when the artist was living at 28 Southampton Row, Bloomsbury.

23

Mandarin Duck*

Aix galericulata (Linnaeus)

Watercolour, and watercolour mixed with gum, $11\frac{1}{16} \times 16$ (28·1 × 40·6)
Signed and dated: *Edward Lear. del. May. 1836.*
Inscribed: *Aix galericulata of Eyton p.119 Dendronessa of Illiger Female. Aix galericulata* (*Linn.*) *China. Male.*

This spectacular species of duck from Eastern Asia was kept in the Knowsley aviaries from early in the 19th century and bred successfully there, but it was not seen by the public until the 1830's when live specimens were first displayed in the London Zoo.

24

Black Tipped or Red Tipped Touraco*

Tauraco macrorhynchus (Fraser)

Watercolour, and watercolour mixed with gum, $16\frac{7}{8} \times 13\frac{15}{16}$ (42·9 × 35·3)
Signed: *Edward Lear. del. July. 1836*
Inscribed: *Corythaix Persa, Linn Corythaix Persa Linn original*

There are two subspecies of *Tauraco macrorhynchus*, one with red, the other with blackish violet tipping to the crest. Lord Derby had both varieties in his aviary but when Lear was at Knowsley they had not been properly distinguished from *Tauraco persa*, to which they are very similar in appearance and for which at that time they were frequently mistaken.

25

Abyssinian Touraco* *Plate 14*

Tauraco leucotis (Rüppell)

Watercolour, and watercolour mixed with gum,
$16\frac{15}{16} \times 13\frac{5}{8}$ (43 × 34·6)
Signed and dated: *Edward Lear del. July. 1836.*
Inscribed: *Corythaix Leucotis Rupp Abyssinia*

Lord Derby received this specimen from John Gould in November 1835. Gould in turn had obtained it from Dr. E. Rüppell, the man who earlier that year had first described the bird to science. There are now two subspecies, one with red tipping to the crest—*Tauraco leucotis donaldsoni*—and the other with greenish violet tipping—*Tauraco leucotis leucotis.*

26

Toco Toucan* *Frontispiece*

Ramphastos toco P.L.S. Müller

Watercolour, and watercolour mixed with gum,
$12\frac{15}{16} \times 20\frac{5}{16}$ (32·8 × 51·6)
Signed and dated: *Edward Lear. del July. 1836.*
Inscribed: *Ramphastos Toco*

This magnificent fruit eating bird was one of many Toucans from South America that Lord Derby maintained in his aviaries. In the early 1830's Lear had gained much valuable experience in the drawing of Toucans when he was engaged by John Gould to produce ten plates for his *Monograph of the Ramphastidæ or Family of Toucans*, published in 1834. In fact, Lear's drawing for Plate 1 of Part 2 of this work depicts a bird of precisely the same species as this.

27

Golden Parakeet* *Plate 11*

Aratinga guarouba (Gmelin)

Watercolour, and watercolour mixed with gum,
$17\frac{15}{16} \times 11\frac{15}{16}$ (44 × 30·3)
Signed and dated: *Edward Lear. del. July. 1836.*
Inscribed: *Conurus luteus Bodd Brazil The same as No. 25*

Lord Derby had two dead specimens of the Golden Parakeet in his museum as well as a live bird in his aviaries, which presumably served as the model for this drawing and died on 17th April 1838.
See no. 11.

28

Orinoco Goose*

Neochen jubata (Spix)

Watercolour, watercolour mixed with gum, and traces of pencil,
$13\frac{3}{16} \times 18\frac{7}{8}$ (33·5 × 47·9)
Signed and dated: *Edward Lear. del. July. 1836.*
Inscribed: *Chenalopex jubata (Spix) Tropical America. The Original of the Plate in the 'Gleanings'.*

The original study for Plate XV in the *Gleanings*.

This species was not described to science until 1825 although there were several specimens living in the Knowsley aviaries as much as five years before this. The strange stance of the two birds on the right was explained by J. E. Gray in the *Gleanings*: "On the approach of a stranger they have a habit of raising their bodies nearly erect, swelling out their breasts, and flapping their wings against the legs of the intruder. They sometimes bend themselves backwards to such an extent, that they appear as if they would fall on their backs".

Lord Derby succeeded in breeding the Orinoco Goose and sent a pair of young birds he had raised at Knowsley to Queen Victoria.

29

Himalayan Mountain Quail†

Ophrysia superciliosa (J. E. Gray)

Watercolour, and watercolour mixed with gum,
$9\frac{1}{2} \times 13\frac{7}{8}$ (24·1 × 35·3)
Signed and dated: *Edward Lear. del. July. 1836.*
Inscribed: *Rollulus superciliosus, Gray. India?. Drawn from specimens in the Knowsley Museum* (*MSS. Cat No. 259*) *The Original of the Plate in the 'Gleanings'.*

The original study for Plate XVI in the *Gleanings*.

Lord Derby purchased these two birds as dead specimens from Mr. Tucker on 1st April 1836. Lear painted them shortly after their arrival at Knowsley, but they were not known to science until 1846 when J. E. Gray published a description of them, accompanied by a lithograph after this drawing, in the *Gleanings*. Only about six birds of this species have ever been collected from their home range in the foothills of the Himalayas. The last living specimen was seen in 1868 and the species is now presumed to be extinct.

30

Finfoot*

Podica senegalensis petersii Hartlaub

Watercolour, and watercolour mixed with gum,
$12\frac{15}{16} \times 18\frac{7}{8}$ (32·9 × 48)
Signed and dated: *Edward Lear. del. July. 1836.*
Inscribed: *Heliornis senegalensis,*

This specimen was collected by Captain Spiller R.N. and reached Knowsley on 11th March 1835. The curiously lobed feet of this bird make it ideally adapted for walking on soft mud.

31

Spectacled Owl*

Plate 16

Pulsatrix perspicillata (Latham)

Watercolour, and watercolour mixed with gum,
$18\frac{1}{2} \times 11\frac{15}{16}$ (46·9 × 30·3)
Signed and dated: *Edward. Lear. del. August. 1836.*
Inscribed: *Spectacled Owl Strix perspicellata*

This beautiful owl, with its very distinctive markings, is one of the finest to be seen in South America. Several dead specimens of this species were obtained for the museum at Knowsley, Lord Stanley paying fifteen shillings for one early in 1828.

32
Dominican Imperial Parrot
Amazona imperialis Richmond

Watercolour, and watercolour mixed with gum,
$17\frac{7}{16} \times 13\frac{1}{8}$ (44·2 × 33·4)
Signed and dated: *March. 1837. Edward Lear. del.*
Inscribed: *Psittacus Augustus Vigors Zool Proc V.4. p. 80 from Life at the Regent's Park*

This species, which is now close to extinction, lives in the rugged mountain forests on the island of Dominica in the West Indies. Lear drew this from a bird in Regent's Park but Lord Derby also had a specimen.

33
Bare Eyed Dove
Columba gymnophtalmos Temminck

Watercolour, watercolour mixed with gum, and traces of pencil,
$15\frac{3}{8} \times 12\frac{1}{16}$ (39 × 30·6)
Signed: *Edward Lear. del. May. 1837.*
Inscribed: *Columba gymnophthalmos Naked Eyed Pigeon.*

This is a bird from the arid coast of South America bordering the Caribbean. Like many of the pigeons from South America it is pinkish brown with white markings on the wing.

34
Blue Crowned Parakeet*
Plate 7

Aratinga acuticauda haemorrhous (Spix)

Watercolour, and watercolour mixed with gum, over pencil,
$16\frac{7}{8} \times 11\frac{3}{8}$ (42·8 × 29)
Inscribed: *Conurus hæmorrhous (Spix.) Brazil.*

The *Aratinga acuticauda* is found only in South America and this particular subspecies is confined to the states of Piauhy and Bahia in Eastern Brazil. Lord Derby received his first specimen of this species from a Mr. Leadbeater in 1835. In 1846 he obtained two more and in 1848 a fourth specimen was acquired from Chile. Sadly, he was unable to procure a live specimen for the Knowsley aviaries.

35
Black Wood Partridge*
Melanoperdix nigra (Vigors)

Watercolour, and watercolour mixed with gum,
$10\frac{3}{8} \times 15\frac{7}{8}$ (26·4 × 40·3)
Signed and dated: *Edward Lear. del. 15. June. 1837.*
Inscribed: *Cryptonyx niger Vigors*

This small and retiring game bird lives amongst the forest undergrowth in Malaysia, Borneo and Sumatra. Here the black male of the species is depicted, the female having brown plumage.

36
Eastern Australian Native "Cat"*
Dasyurus quoll (Zimmerman)

Watercolour, and watercolour mixed with gum,
$8\frac{5}{16} \times 12\frac{1}{8}$ (20·8 × 30·8)
Signed *E. Lear. del* and dated *Novbr. 1834.*
Inscribed: *Dasyurus Mangei Mas*

This species is found only in remnant pockets in South East Australia and on the island of Tasmania.

The specimen from which Lear drew was almost certainly the one recorded in the Catalogue of Mammals in the Knowsley Museum. This had previously been living in the aviaries but died on 8th July 1836.

37
Dourouocouli or Night Monkey

Plate 15

Aotes trivirgatus Humboldt

Watercolour, watercolour mixed with gum, and traces of pencil, $18\frac{1}{2} \times 12\frac{3}{4}$ (47 × 32·4)
Signed and dated: *August. 1835 Edward Lear del.*
Inscribed: *Nyctipithecus felinus, Spix. South America. The Original of the Plate in the 'Gleanings'*

The original study for Plate I in the *Gleanings.*

This species is widely distributed throughout the forests of Central and South America, where this specimen was obtained. Five examples of this species are listed in the Catalogue of the Mammals in the Knowsley Museum, though none of these is recorded as having been alive in the menagerie, which again throws doubt on Gray's assertion in the *Gleanings* that all the illustrations there are "representations of *living* specimens".

An earlier preliminary study for this drawing in the Houghton Library of Harvard University allows an interesting insight into Lear's method of work, which he must have applied to all of his zoological illustrations. Drawn in ink and watercolour over initial essays with the pencil, it abounds with artist's references and experimental watercolour tests, a procedure that was necessitated by the scientific precision required in the finished work.

38
Nile Soft-Shelled Turtle
Trionyx triunguis (Forskål)

Watercolour, watercolour mixed with gum, and brown ink outline, $18\frac{1}{16} \times 12\frac{3}{8}$ (46 × 31·5)
Signed and dated: *Edwd. Lear. del. May. 1836.*
Inscribed: *upper side Tyrse Argus, Gray Western Africa. Brought home, alive, by Mr. Whitfield. The Original of the figure in the 'Gleanings'.*

The original study for Plate XVII in the *Gleanings.*

This specimen was brought home alive from Western Africa by Mr. Whitfield and it lived for some time in the pond in Knowsley Park. On its death it was presented to the British Museum. Its markings are rather distinctive, consisting of black-edged yellow streaks on the side of its head, and numerous eyed spots on the top of its soft shell.

39
Nile Soft-Shelled Turtle
Trionyx triunguis (Forskål)

Watercolour, watercolour mixed with gum, and ink outline, $18\frac{1}{16} \times 12\frac{3}{8}$ ($46 \times 31{\cdot}5$)
Signed and dated: *Edwd. Lear. del. May. 1836*
Inscribed: *lower side Tyrse Argus, Gray. Western Africa. Brought home, alive, by Mr. Whitfield.*

The underside of no. 38.

40
Malayan Giant Squirrel*
Plate 18
Ratufa bicolor (Sparrman)

Watercolour, and watercolour mixed with gum, $12\frac{3}{16} \times 19\frac{7}{16}$ ($30{\cdot}9 \times 49{\cdot}4$)
Signed and dated: *Edward Lear. del. July. 1836.*
Inscribed: *Sciurus Javensis, Schreb. India. The Original of the figure in the 'Gleanings'.*

The original study for Plate VI in the *Gleanings*.

Lord Derby had three examples of this species on display in his menagerie at Knowsley. This particular specimen was alive when Lear drew it, but it died not long afterwards on 27th December 1836. This species is one of four in the genus, which has a wide distribution throughout the Far East.

41
Banded Mongoose
Mungos mungo (Gmelin)

Watercolour, and watercolour mixed with gum, $11\frac{7}{16} \times 19\frac{7}{16}$ ($29{\cdot}1 \times 49{\cdot}3$)
Signed: *Edward Lear. del.* and dated *Novembr. 1836*
Inscribed: *Mungos fasciatus, (Desm.) River Gambia, Western Africa. The Original of the plate in the 'Gleanings'.*

The original study for Plate V in the *Gleanings*.

Like no. 38, this specimen was brought back alive from Africa by Mr. Whitfield, who found it in Gambia. From all accounts, the species had a very extensive distribution: Dr. Rüppell found it in Abyssinia, Captain Clapperton near Lake Tschad, Colonel Perronet Thompson in Sierra Leone and Dr. A. Smith and others in the interior of South Africa. Lord Derby owned two specimens, and the one that Whitfield brought home died in his menagerie on 26th May 1835.

42
Chimpanzee
Plate 26
Pan troglodytes (Blumenbach)

Watercolour and pencil, $5\frac{7}{8} \times 3\frac{3}{4}$ ($14{\cdot}8 \times 9{\cdot}4$)
Signed: *Lear. del.*
Inscribed: *Anthropithecus Troglodytes (Linn.) Western Africa.*

This drawing of a chimp, dressed up and playing with a hoop, is unique among the other zoological illustrations. It perhaps records a favourite pet at Knowsley.

43
Lake Lugano

Watercolour, $4\frac{1}{8} \times 8$ (10·4 × 20·3)
Signed in monogram: *EL*

Lear was a life-long sufferer from asthma and in 1837 his illness was so acute that the 13th Earl of Derby and his nephew, Robert Hornby, offered to send him to Rome where he might recover his health and have an opportunity to paint. On his way Lear stopped in Milan and set out on a walking tour of Como and Lugano. When he returned to Milan a fortnight later his sketch-books were full of ideas that he subsequently worked up into highly finished watercolours such as this, which was almost certainly executed late in his career.

44
Mount Soratte

Watercolour, $4\frac{1}{8} \times 8$ (10·4 × 20·3)
Signed in monogram: *EL*
Inscribed: *in a form of Greek, Soracte* (?).

Lear finally arrived in Rome in December 1837 and he remained there for over ten years, during which time he returned to England only twice, in 1841 to publish *Views in Rome and its Environs* and in 1845/46 to supervise publication of his *Illustrated Excursions in Italy* and the celebrated *Book of Nonsense*.

One of his favourite haunts near Rome was the mountainous terrain to the North. Here he came on numerous occasions to make sketches of Mount Soratte, an isolated limestone peak in the Apennines, which is clearly visible from the city. It was on these sketches that Lear later based this watercolour view.

A note in pencil on the back of the frame reads: *Received at Knowsley 17/5/81*

45
Magliano

Pen and brown ink, coloured washes and gouache, heightened with white, $10\frac{3}{4} \times 16\frac{5}{8}$ (27·3 × 42·1), cut at the corners.
Inscribed: *Magliano.* and *August 23. 1843.*

Magliano dei Marsi, to distinguish it from other Italian towns named Magliano, is situated in the Abruzzi eighty miles E.N.E. of Rome. Lear arrived there during his second tour of the Kingdom of Naples on 22nd August 1843 and stayed for three days.

In the first volume of his *Illustrated Excursions in Italy*, which he dedicated to Edward, Lord Stanley (Vol. II was dedicated to Edward, Earl of Derby), Lear wrote: "We passed beneath Scurcola, as when K. [Charles Knight] and I were together; then, leaving the road to Avezzano, we soon arrived at Magliano, a most neat and thriving little town, containing fifteen hundred inhabitants, placed on an isolated eminence below the towering Monte Velino, and commanding views over the whole of the Campi Valentini".

A view of Magliano from the same spot, but with mules and additional staffage figures in the foreground, appears as a litho-graph on plate 16 of Vol. I of *Illustrated Excursions in Italy*.

46
Tufo

Pen and brown ink, and watercolour, heightened with white, 17 × 12½ (43·1 × 31·7), cut at the corners.
Inscribed: *Tufo. 12. October. 1843.*

This watercolour drawing was made while Lear was staying in Tufo, in the Abruzzi, with his friend, Baron Coletti, a wealthy landowner who had property there. Lear stayed with him from 11th to 16th October, passing all of these days "rather idly". "Tufo", wrote Lear, "consists of three villages . . . Tufo Alto, the smallest, on the brow of a hill; Tufo proper, a clean little town in the valley and Villa Tufo, a third hamlet at a little distance".

47
Passerano

Pen and ink, with some pencil outlines and coloured washes, 6⅞ × 15¼ (17·5 × 38·7)
Inscribed: *Passerano. 20. October. 1843.*
Also with colour notes and other notations.

Lear concluded his second tour through the Kingdom of Naples shortly after visiting Tufo and on 17th October 1843 he set out for Rome. On his way back he stopped briefly in Passerano, a town to the North of the Via Prenestina between Tivoli and Praeneste, and went out into the countryside to sketch.

As is the case with other Lear drawings of this type, the presence of colour notes and other *aide-mémoires* is an almost certain indication that this particular watercolour view was made on the spot. The fact that the artist made no attempt to paint over or otherwise disguise these notations suggests that the picture was not intended for sale.

48
Passerano

Pen and ink, with some pencil outlines and coloured washes, heightened with white, 7½ × 15½ (19·1 × 39·2)
Inscribed: *Passerano. 20. October. 1843.*

The same hill town as no. 47 and drawn the same day, but from a different vantage point further along the valley.
See no. 47.

49
A Classical Ruin on the Via Nomentana

Watercolour, 9½ × 16 (24·1 × 40·5)
Inscribed: *Via di Porta Nomentana. Decembr. 23. 1843*

Lear was unaccustomed to travelling far from Rome during the winter months and this watercolour sketch was most likely executed on one of the many short excursions that he made out of the city.

Roman ruins like this abound on the Via Nomentana, a road which leaves Rome by Michelangelo's Porta Pia and follows the line of the ancient consular road to Nomentum, now called Mentana, 13 miles to the North East.

50

Ióannina

Plate 23

Watercolour, $6\frac{1}{4} \times 10$ ($15 \cdot 8 \times 25 \cdot 4$)
Signed in monogram: *EL*

Ióannina, Janina or Yannina, is a town on the western shore of Lake Yannina on the mainland of Greece. Lear arrived there on horseback from Zítka on 5th November 1848 and, recalling the occasion, noted in his journal: "The first feeling with which I gazed on it (Ióannina) was nearly akin to disappointment—perhaps from the extreme bareness of the surrounding hills, and the too unbroken line of Mitzekéli, the great mountain which forms one side of the landscape. There lay the peninsula stretching far into the dark grey water, with its mosque, its cypress tufts, and fortress walls . . . there was the fatal island, the closing scene of the history of the once all-powerful Alí [Ali Pasha, the 'Lion of Ióannina']".

Lear passed through Ióannina again on 4th May 1849.

51

Philae

Plate 21

Watercolour, $6\frac{1}{2} \times 10\frac{1}{4}$ ($16 \cdot 5 \times 26$)
Signed in monogram: *EL*

In 1854 and 1867 Lear took part in expeditions up the Nile. On the first occasion he and his party encamped for several days on the island of Philae, a beautiful haven of temples and palm trees. To his sister, Ann, he wrote: "It is impossible to describe the place any further than by saying it is more like a real *fairy island* than anything else I can compare it to. It is very small, & was formerly all covered with temples, of which the ruins of 5 or 6 now only remain. The great T. of Isis, on the terrace of which I am now writing, is so extremely wonderful that no words can give the least idea of it".

52

Corfu

Plate 22

Pen and brown ink, with coloured washes,
$13\frac{3}{4} \times 20\frac{3}{8}$ ($34 \cdot 8 \times 51 \cdot 8$)
Inscribed: *Corfù. 15. Feby. 5.P.M.* Also with colour notes.

Lear visited Corfu for the first time in 1848 at the invitation of George Bowen, rector of the university, when the Ionian Isles were still under British protection. He was so enchanted by the island and its inhabitants that he twice made his home there, from 1855 to 1858, and again from 1861 to 1864. He returned, for the last time, in 1877.

This landscape study was probably made during Lear's second stay on Corfu, possibly in 1856, when he is known to have spent much of February sketching on the island.

53

Olive Grove on Corfu

Plate 19

Watercolour, $12\frac{1}{4} \times 19\frac{1}{2}$ ($31 \cdot 1 \times 49 \cdot 4$)
Inscribed: *Decr 27–29 /55—Jany 1. /56* and numbered *10*

In this picture Corfu is seen from above the nearby village of Ascension. With various modifications and embellishments Lear painted several versions of this same view and it occurs as the first of twenty lithographic plates in his *Views in the Seven Ionian Islands*, published in 1863.

54
Jerusalem

Watercolour, 7 × $14\frac{3}{4}$ (17·8 × 37·5)
Signed in monogram: *EL*
Inscribed: *Jerusalem 1858, from Mt of Olives.*

Lear arrived in Jerusalem towards the end of March, 1858. In May he wrote to his friend and patron, Lady Waldegrave: "O my nose! O my eyes! O my feet! How you all suffered in that vile place! for let me tell you, physically Jerusalem is the foulest and odiousest place on earth . . . and your memories of its interior are but horrid dreams of squalor & filth, clamour & uneasiness, hatred & malice & all uncharitableness. But the outside is full of melancholy glory, exquisite beauty & a world of past history of all ages:— every point forcing you to think on a vastly dim receding past, or a time of Roman war & splendour, (for Ælia Capitolium was a fine city) or a smash of Moslem & Crusader years, with long long dull winter of deep decay through centuries of misrule. The Arab & his sheep are alone the wanderers on the pleasant vallies and breezy hills round Zion:— the file of slow camels all that brings to mind the commerce of Tyre & other bygone merchandize".

55
Paxos

Watercolour, heightened with white,
$6\frac{1}{2}$ × $10\frac{1}{4}$ (16·5 × 26)
Signed in monogram: *EL*

Paxos lies off the western coast of Greece in the Ionian Sea just south of Corfu. Lear had first toured the Ionian Islands in 1848 and he returned there in 1863 for an eight weeks' stay. During this time he filled a large portfolio with landscape sketches and on his return to England he started work on his Ionian book, completing twenty lithographs and writing brief accompanying descriptive notes. The outcome of this labour, *Views in the Seven Ionian Islands*, was published in December 1863 with a dedication to the Lord High Commissioner, Sir Henry Storks. This watercolour, or at least the preliminary sketches for it, presumably dates from this period.

56
A Rocky Inlet on the Island of Paxos *Plate 20*

Pen and brown ink, washed with watercolour,
$13\frac{5}{8}$ × $19\frac{1}{2}$ (34·5 × 49·5)
Inscribed: *Rocks of Pio . . . li* (?) *Paxõ. 7. April 1863* and numbered (*12.*). Also with extensive notations.

This watercolour is one of the series that Lear produced during the spring of 1863 with a view to possible publication in his projected volume of *Views in the Seven Ionian Islands*.

The coast of Paxos is indented with many small inlets such as this and here, as on other occasions, Lear was especially fascinated by the way that reflections from the water cast bright colours on to the adjacent cliffs which "tho in shade, are all light off sea".

57
Santa Maura

Pen and brown ink, with blue and beige washes, heightened with white, $14\frac{1}{2}$ × 21 (36·7 × 53·3)
Inscribed: *Santa Maura 12–13. April. 1863.* and numbered *29.*

Also inscribed with colour notes and other notations.

Like no. 56, this was drawn during the course of Lear's travels in the Ionian Islands in April and May 1863.

Also known as Leukas and sometimes identified with ancient Ithaca, Santa Maura lies off Acarnania in the Ionian Sea, S.E. of Corfu.

See no. 55.

58
Cattaro (Kotor) *Plate 25*

Heavy watercolour over pen and ink, heightened with white, 11 × 17¾ (27·9 × 34·5)
Signed in monogram: *EL*

April 1866 found Lear in the seaport of Cattaro on the Bay of Kotor in Dalmatia, whither he had sailed after his departure from Malta. The medieval town, dwarfed by the surrounding mountains, seems to have rivetted Lear's interest for he drew it at least five times from the same view-point across the bay, making sure always to focus attention on the wildly zigzagging road leading up to Cetinje.

As was often his practice, Lear later referred to these sketches when he was engaged on this watercolour view of Kotor some five years later.

A label on the back of the frame reads: *Cáttaro in Dalmatia from drawings made on the spot 1866 Edward Lear 1871.* (*The Earl of Derby. Knowsley Hall. near Liverpool*)

59
The Forest of Bavella, Corsica *Plate 24*

Watercolour, heightened with white,
11⅜ × 18 (28·9 × 45·7)
Signed in monogram: *EL*

Early in 1868, with several travel journals already completed and awaiting a publisher, Lear decided to set out for Corsica to gather material for yet another book. There, on 28th April, he climbed to the top of the pass known as the Bocca di Larone and feasted his eyes for the first time on the towering pines and lofty peaks of the Forest of Bavella, which he likened to "a vast amphitheatre . . . exceeding in grandeur anything of the kind I have ever seen".

60
The Plain of Delhi

Watercolour, 4 × 8 (10·2 × 20·3)
Signed in monogram: *EL*
Inscribed: *Delhi*

On the invitation of the Viceroy, Lord Northbrook, Lear set out for India in October, 1873. He had received several commissions for Indian landscapes and Delhi was but one of countless cities on an exhausting itinerary that kept him constantly on the move for fourteen months. During his sojourn in India Lear often felt ill and depressed and to dispel this depression he composed long, nonsensical letters to his friends, describing his activities in a string of puns. He remained in Delhi ten days, "a making Delhineations of the Delhicate architecture as is all impressed on my mind as inDelhibly as the Delhiterious quality of the water in that city".

61
Sparta

Heavy watercolour, $12\frac{3}{4} \times 20\frac{3}{8}$ ($32{\cdot}3 \times 51{\cdot}7$)
Signed in monogram: *EL* and dated *1880*
Inscribed: *Sparta 1849*

After visiting Cairo, Suez, Sinai and Malta earlier in the year, Lear returned to Greece in March 1849. Towards the end of the month he was in the region near Sparta and Leondari, sketching again from nature.

This view, another of his highly finished late watercolours, seems—from the date and inscription in the bottom left corner—to depend on earlier drawings done at that time. It shows the modern town of Sparta seen from the scanty ruins of the ancient city just to the South.

62
Suli

Heavy watercolour, heightened with white, $12\frac{5}{8} \times 20\frac{1}{8}$ (32×51)
Signed in monogram: *EL* and dated *1881*
Inscribed: *Suli*

Lear based this watercolour on drawings he had made during his travels in Albania and Illyria in 1849, when on 5th May he actually spent the night in the fortress of Suli-Kastro, which is shown here.

Lear's manservant, Giorgio Kokali, who accompanied the artist on many of his journeys, was of Suliote origin. In their fight against Turkish oppression the Suliotes had fought successfully against Ali Pasha, Turkish governor of Ióannina (see no. 50), between 1790 and 1802 but many of them were massacred in 1803 after he had tricked them into a false truce.

A lithotint depicting the fortress of Suli-Kastro features as plate 17 in Lear's *Journals of a Landscape Painter in Albania Etc.*

26 Chimpanzee (No. 42)